The Greatest of These is LOVE

TANICA JACKSON

www.TrueVinePublishing.org

The Greatest of These is Love
By Tanica Jackson

Published by True Vine Publishing Company
P.O. Box 22448
Nashville, TN. 37202
www.TrueVinePublishing.org

Copyright © 2021 by Tanica Jackson
ISBN: 978-1-7357540-7-9

All rights reserved. No part of this book may be reproduced in any form or by any electronic or mechanical means, including information storage without permission in writing from the publisher. Scripture quotations taken from the Holy Bible, American Standard Version.

Cover Design by: K. Luxe Services LLC.

Headshot by: P. Scott Photography

Printing in the United States of America — First Printing

For more information about the author or to book the author to speak, contact: www.TanicaJackson.com

PREFACE
1 CORINTHIANS 13 ASV

1 *If I speak with the tongues of men and of angels, but have not love, I am become sounding brass, or a clanging cymbal.*
2 *And if I have the gift of prophecy, and know all mysteries and all knowledge; and if I have all faith, so as to remove mountains, but have not love, I am nothing.*
3 *And if I bestow all my goods to feed the poor, and if I give my body to be burned, but have not love, it profiteth me nothing.*
4 *Love suffereth long, and is kind; love envieth not; love vaunteth not itself, is not puffed up,*
5 *doth not behave itself unseemly, seeketh not its own, is not provoked, taketh not account of evil;*
6 *rejoiceth not in unrighteousness, but rejoiceth with the truth;*
7 *beareth all things, believeth all things, hopeth all things, endureth all things.*
8 *Love never faileth: but whether there be prophecies, they shall be done away; whether there be tongues, they shall cease; whether there be knowledge, it shall be done away.*
9 *For we know in part, and we prophesy in part;*
10 *but when that which is perfect is come, that which is in part shall be done away.*
11 *When I was a child, I spake as a child, I felt as a child, I thought as a child: now that I am become a man, I have put away childish things.*
12 *For now we see in a mirror, darkly; but then face to face: now I know in part; but then shall I know fully even as also I was fully known.*
13 *But now abideth faith, hope, love, these three;* **and the greatest of these is love.**

INSPIRATION

There is no difficulty that enough love will not conquer; no disease that love will not heal; no door that enough love will not open. It makes no difference how deeply set the trouble; how hopeless the outlook; how muddled the tangle; how great the mistake. A sufficient realization of love will dissolve it all. If only you could love enough, you would be the happiest and most powerful being in the world.

~ Emmet Fox

"*If there's a book you really want to read but it hasn't been written yet, then you must write it.*"

~ Toni Morrison

Healers are spiritual warriors who have found the courage to defeat the darkness of their souls. Awakening and rising from the depths of their fears like a Phoenix rising from the ashes. Reborn with a wisdom and strength that creates a light that shines bright enough to help encourage and inspire others out of their own darkness.

~ Unknown

I believe that we all have major gifts and talents embedded within us that God is ready to reveal, but some of those talents will never see the light of day if we continue to hold on to negative self-talk, limiting beliefs and unforgiveness. So, I encourage you to examine yourself. Let go of the things that are preventing your growth and expansion and live in God's purpose.

~Tanica Jackson

DEDICATION

Revelations 12:12 "and they overcame him by the blood of the Lamb, and by the word of their testimony."

This book is dedicated to the underdog, the one who always seems to have it especially rough. The ones who have always been rejected no matter how great a person they are. I wrote this book to inspire you to consciously take a look within in order to identify those things that are not serving your highest good and to graciously release them. I wrote this book to let you know that you are loved and valued and to give you the courage to pursue your life's purpose. I wrote this book to let you know that God will restore you and give you the biggest comeback of your life. Just keep going. It's time to heal.

Dedicated to my amazing children Eric, Ariel, and Adam. Never be afraid to speak your truth, Love yourself and Follow your dreams.

TABLE OF CONTENTS

In the Beginning, There Was Me 9

Stolen Innocence 11

The *Silence* Killer 16

Make Room 20

From Dream Life to Nightmare 24

A Double Life 29

200 Months 35

Everything Has to Change 41

Confirmation 54

No More Chaos 58

A Quest for God 61

Love Me, First! 70

Freedom 75

Miracles 77

Reconciliation 82

The Golden Veil 86

Afterword 95

Pledges and Affirmations 96

IN THE BEGINNING, THERE WAS ME

I was seven years old when a question came to my mind that would nag me for the next three decades. I was watching Saturday-morning cartoons when the question arose out of thin air. *Who am I? What is my purpose?*

What seven-year-old child contemplates such thoughts? For years, I have battled with this question, and for years, it seems dark and evil forces in my life have tried to prevent me from discovering the answer. This story, although it is far from complete, is how I discovered who I am and why God put me on this earth.

My story began somewhat normal. For my first nine years, life was fun growing up on the south side of Chicago. I was in church seemingly all of the time, and I participated in all of the after school activities. My mother did everything that she could do to keep my sister, my two brothers and I together. We had a small but very close knit family. When you saw my siblings and I, you also saw my cousins.

My family had a great time hanging out together. We would go on family trips, to the park, you name it. My mom was on board for whatever we wanted to do for fun, as long as we were safe. I liked music early on. I sang every time I had a chance. It was my outlet. I was still shy, but at a moment's notice, I could shed my quiet exterior and express myself easily through song. Singing meant everything to me. There was no shortage of good music in my house. My mother had excellent taste in music. She introduced me to some of the greats like Luther Vandross, Anita Baker and Miki Howard.

One summer, we had planned to visit the taste of Chicago. My mother set things up where I could sing for the crowd. It was my largest audience. I remember it like it was yesterday. I had gotten up on stage and immediately got stage fright. I was shaking and even tried to exit stage left. The crowd kept cheering me on telling me to go ahead and sing. I was so scared that I turned my back on the crowd and belted out an Anita Baker tune. The crowd loved me. I received a roaring applause, and this tremendously boosted my confidence. I went on to sing in several community choirs throughout the city.

I was a quiet child most of the time, but I was always observing. I was definitely a people watcher and a thinker. I would analyze people based on how they acted or the things they would say. I have had a gift of discernment for as long as I could remember. Unfortunately, my discernment could not protect me from what was to come one summer night.

STOLEN INNOCENCE

*W*hen I was ten, my mom and dad moved into separate houses. I wasn't quite sure why they separated, but I was super happy because this was the very first time that I had my own room. For as long as I can remember, I shared rooms with my older brother and sister. I finally had a chance to decorate and show my individual taste, so I collected posters of my favorite Disney characters and my favorite basketball team, the Chicago Bulls, and plastered them all over my walls. My mom wasn't completely thrilled because it was a brand new house, and I had completely covered every single wall in my bedroom with art and posters.

My bedroom was my safe haven; it was where I created everything! I wrote my first song there; I would journal there; it was where I got some of my brightest ideas and where I felt most productive. My bedroom window faced the front yard, so I would turn off my bedroom light and get a good look at who was coming and going. It was the perfect room for watching everything that happened in the front of the house. There was one man in particular that my mom dated by the name of Tony. My first impression of Tony was that he was kind of weird.

Tony visibly looked like he had been through a lot by the time he entered into my mother's life. Tony was one of the new boy toys my mom was playing with. She had reentered the dating scene after splitting from my father. She didn't announce that she was dating, but we noticed the different men who would pick her up from the house to take her on dates. My mom's dating was ok with me. Besides, she is a beautiful woman deserving of love, so why not?

Of all the guys mom dated, for some reason, Tony stuck. He had a scar that spanned from one ear to the other as if someone had tried to cut his neck. I never asked my mother what had happened to him, but I assumed that she knew. Tony didn't have much personality. He didn't try too hard to impress us. I really didn't know what to even say to him. My mother had dated several men over the course of my life, so I just figured that he would be around for a little while and then soon be gone like the others.

Tony's eyes were cold, and it seemed like he had a lot on his mind all the time. He would often spend nights at our house, and soon, he moved in. It didn't take long to see Tony for who he truly was. This man was very manipulative, and he clearly had his own agenda for our household. He had my mother's head in the clouds. After a few months, he was ready to make his move and assume the role as man of our household.

One summer night, my twin sister and I stayed up late watching television. I slept in my twin sister's bedroom that night. She had bunk beds in her room, and on this night I slept on the top bunk. Shortly after my twin and I fell asleep, Tony entered my sister's room and picked me up out of the top bunk and carried me into my bedroom. My first thought was that he was carrying me to my room so that I could sleep in my own bed, but I was wrong. Instead, he pulled my underwear down and began to sexually assault me. I wanted to scream, but nothing would come out. During the assault, he told me if I made a sound he would kill my family, and I believed him.

I can still envision him on top of me and the orange glare from the streetlight shining through my bedroom window highlighting the scar on his neck. This incident changed me forever. I wasn't the same naive little girl I had once been. It broke me into a million pieces. My innocence had been snatched away from me right in the place that I called home. I really didn't have time to process what had happened to me. I had to grow up really fast and become responsible because I couldn't let this happen to my sister.

The next day, my mom talked to us again about Tony moving into our house. I couldn't have that happen after what he had done to me. I was still afraid that he would keep his promise and murder my family, but I had to speak up. As my mother was talking I blurted out,

"He raped me!"

My mother was crushed. She went from being hurt to being angry.

"I want him dead!" She screamed.

My mother and I sat on the foot of her queen bed and cried in each other's arms. She apologized for what happened to me profusely. My mother called the police, and I was rushed to the hospital where the doctors conducted a rape kit on me. There were police officers there who questioned me over and over about what had happened. I cried a whole lot because as a young ten-year-old girl, I was thrown into the light of the truth that people in this world were evil.

It took two years, but I would have my day in court to testify against Tony. By the time I was twelve, I took the stand in an Illinois courtroom and testified against him. I came face to face with the monster who had stolen my innocence right in the place I called home. The judge instructed me to identify the man who assaulted me. I was so afraid to look in his direction. The look in his eyes was so cold and evil. I was sure that he would lunge over the tables and chairs that separated us and make good on his promise to kill me.

The judge had to reassure me several times that I was safe. Once I began to speak, I just couldn't stop talking. The attorney who questioned me asked me to provide a detailed account of what happened that night. I cried as I told the judge and everyone in the courtroom how Tony raped me. After I was done with my testimony, a feeling of emptiness fell over me. I honestly felt so unprotected and vulnerable. After a two-hour recess, the court reconvened. My mother and I went back into the courtroom for the verdict.

"We find the defendant... Guilty."

I was young and didn't understand most of what I was hearing in that courtroom, but that one word was all I needed to hear. *Guilty.*

Tony was found guilty of rape and received three years in prison. When the sentence was handed down, there was a calm that came over me for a moment. I felt like everything could now be placed behind me and that I could move on with my life. Unfortunately, that was short lived. When I returned home, I would become engulfed in fear. Although Tony was in jail, his shadow loomed over me. I never felt safe.

THE *SILENCE* KILLER

*F*ear filled my mind, body and spirit after Tony was imprisoned. I thought I would be free, but little did I know, a new prison awaited me-- a prison of fear and silence. I was afraid because Tony was a local man from my neighborhood. He had friends and family who lived in our neighborhood and walked our streets. I was fearful of retaliation. I had to walk to and from school, and we continued to live in the same house.

On top of that, I would find that my one defender in this process—my mother—would force me to put on the shackles of silence. She would tell me to stop talking about the incident.

"It's over. He's in jail. Enough is enough," she said.

She wanted me to forget about it and just throw it out of my mind. She specifically asked me not to mention anything about the rape to my father. She did not want him to know anything about the situation. *Why wouldn't she want me to tell my father?* I wondered.

My mother led me to believe that talking about the situation was not of benefit, and she wanted to let it go. It's as if she believed the guilty verdict erased all that was done, and life would go back to normal. But life would never be the same for me ever again, and neither would it be the same for her.

My mother wanted me to act as if I was able to magically forget about being raped, but I thought that she was doing what was best for me. Besides, my mother was doing the best that she could as a single parent, and she thought it would be best that I moved on and didn't talk to my father about anything that had happened. So, that's what I did.

The following week, I went to school as if nothing happened. I tried really hard to adjust; but the more I tried, the more I became disconnected from who I was. I felt like I didn't have a voice anymore, like my mouth had been sewn shut. My mother did to me what Tony tried to do--keep me from seeking help. She didn't understand that my mind and body would not simply erase the trauma it experienced. She did not understand how badly I needed to talk about what I experienced. Instead, she imprisoned me in a cell of silence.

From that point until my father's death, I suffered in that cell. Seeing and talking to him but not being able to tell him what had happened to me was so stressful. I was so stressed, my hair began to turn gray. I tried to reconcile this situation in my head by convincing myself that I had done everything I was supposed to do. I mean, I told my mom what happened. She called the police. The bad guy was arrested and had gone to prison. So why couldn't I get over it? I wondered. I resolved in my head that everything we did was sufficient to call the issue resolved. I was the victim in this situation. I did nothing wrong, but at the same time, I felt very guilty.

I knew that if I had been given the opportunity to tell my father everything that happened, he would have been angry with my mom. I mean, I had to live with her. I had no idea what her reaction would be and what would happen to me as a result. I didn't want her relationship with my dad to be more strained than it already was so, I decided to suppress everything! I got into art, singing, dancing, and anything else I could, just to forget.

By forcing me to hide this incident from my father, I learned the behavior of omitting the truth. By forcing me to live a life of omission with my father, I began to live my life that way. I felt like if I was silent about a situation, then it never happened. I was extremely passive, which lasted well into my late thirties. It shaped the foundation for other relationships I allowed in my life.

When traumatic things happened in my family, we would never openly discuss them. We quietly swept our dirt under the rug and moved on silently from one traumatic experience to the next, ignoring any process of healing. I knew that some of the things I saw and experienced in my younger years were very wrong. I knew that when I got older I would do better. I knew exactly who and what I didn't want to be.

I would hide from anything that seemed like it could result in conflict. I allowed myself to be bullied by a few of the neighborhood girls. I ran from conflict, and it seemed like I just began to steamroll from one existential crisis to the next.

The effects of hiding this trauma had an impact on us all. My mother's drinking got worse. She would drink and then yell and even physically beat and punish us. I later found out that she was suffering with substance abuse. I could remember one day my mother lying sick on the couch in the living room. She suffered as she shivered from the chills and poured sweat as the chills turned to hot flashes, accompanied by endless puking. I thought she was just sick with the flu or something but when I grew older it dawned on me that she was actually going through withdrawals.

Silence was killing us slowly. I didn't know if I would survive it's grasp, but something inside of me told me that there would come a day where my Mother and I would reconcile.

MAKE ROOM

Some years had gone by since Tony had gone to jail, and I seemed to have gotten back to some form of normality in my life. I had a group of childhood friends that I would hang around in the neighborhood. We all went to the same school. A few girls and I had formed a singing group. We didn't officially have a group name, but we were always together. You really didn't see one of us without the other. Life was fun again.

I was with my tight group of friends when I met Dwayne. Dwayne was super cute. He was a "PK"-- Preacher's kid. He stayed well dressed, always wore a collar shirt, and had so much confidence and charisma about himself. Dwayne and I took a liking to one another and started "talking" when I was in the 7th grade.

He went to a private school so when they had days off he would walk to my school and walk me home. He was a nice boy who came from a seemingly good family. He lived with both his parents and had three little sisters. They appeared to be the perfect family. I had only read about families like his in books and saw something similar to it on television. His mom welcomed me into the family and would include me on trips they took to Great America. I was one of them. I felt like I had escaped the hell that I called home.

Dwayne had gone to high school a year ahead of me. I was supposed to go to Kenwood Academy on the south side; but at the last minute, I decided to go to the same school that he attended. I wanted to be close to him, so I followed him to high school. I didn't tell him that I would be attending his school. I just showed up on the first day. He was so surprised, but always the gentleman. He welcomed me with open arms and showed me around.

High school was a challenge for me. I struggled to fit in and would drift from one group of friends to another trying to find my place. It was a rough time, my grades struggle, and my friends were a terrible influence on me. I was smoking weed and cigarettes and just doing what I thought was acceptable to the masses, being a mindless follower.

When Dwayne found out about me smoking, he confronted me and told me that if I didn't stop smoking that he would have nothing to do with me. I liked him a lot, so I complied. No one had ever expressed this much interest in me to try to stop me from going down the wrong path. It made me like him even more. During my junior year of high school, we dated seriously, and I got pregnant with our first child. As the pregnancy progressed things began to grow tense at home between my mother and I.

My relationship with my mother was extremely strained. I resented her for the proverbial gag order she imposed upon me, and I'll admit that I would hang the abuse of the man she allowed in our home over her head.

I know that she suffered from the guilt of what happened and displaced that guilt towards me. Perhaps my presence was a constant reminder of her biggest mistake. We didn't know how to deal with our emotions.

One night my mother began to really stress me about doing chores in the house. I felt like my mom hated me and would find reasons to pick on me. I was a young mother with a small child, so I guess I wasn't moving as quickly as she wanted.

"Get in here and clean these damn dishes!" She yelled.

I had to take care of my son first. Before I could finish up with my son, my mom burst into the room screaming and swinging. Although I was her child and still a dependent, I was also a mother. I was not going to allow my son to witness her abuse. I respected my mother and would not hit her back, but I'd had enough. I packed my bags, took my son, and left.

I didn't know where I was going to go, but I knew I was getting out of that house. How could the person who used to be my role model and idol become my biggest enemy? I cried as I drove off in my red Pontiac Grand Am. As I sped away from my mother's house, I decided to go to the only place I knew where my son and I would be loved-- Dwayne and his family. I was so relieved to walk into their open and welcoming arms. They opened their doors to me without hesitation and made room for us.

My mother never really supported any of my dreams. We no longer had the regular mother-daughter talks, but she and my twin sister did. At times, I would try to offer an olive branch and get my mother to take road trips with me, but she always declined. However, she would always make the seven-hour drive to visit my sister. It made me feel as if she did not care enough to show the slightest bit of interest in me. In return, I began to distance myself from her and drew closer to Dwayne and his family.

Dwayne and I worked full-time jobs. We finished high school at our respective times; and a few years later, Dwayne and I welcomed our second child into the world. Our family continued to grow. I was so happy to be with Dwayne. He was an amazing father to our children. My trust in men was finally being restored, and in 2003, Dwayne and I got married at the Cook County courthouse. We seemed to have a good life together. We were working and raising our family together. This was the family that I felt like I had always been missing.

While I was in Lala Land, the reality of my family's foundation was almost ready to reveal itself to me. Everything between Dwayne and I would suddenly change for the worst.

FROM DREAM LIFE TO NIGHTMARE

*O*ver the years, Dwayne and I went from being best friends to husband and wife. I will admit that I had become complacent in the marriage and started to get comfortable. Dwayne began working a night job as a bouncer at a local nightclub, and I was always either at work or at home with our children. We began to grow apart at a rapid pace. With the type of work Dwayne did at the time, there was never a shortage of beautiful women around at any given time; and soon, my best friend had begun to morph into a different person.

Our marriage endured countless infidelities and physical fights. There was one instance where I walked into Dwayne's place of business and saw him very cozy with a mutual female friend of ours. She was so desperate for love and wanted to be included so badly that she was willing to pose as my friend so she could spend time around Dwayne. She wanted to be close to me so that she could learn my mannerisms and how I operated my day-to-day life. It was like some fatal attraction stuff. She was at the kids' birthdays, family functions— the whole nine yards.

When I saw them together, I blacked out and began swinging at his head with my keys in my hand. My keys scraped his eyes and scratched his cornea causing him to lose his sight. I didn't intentionally mean to injure him, but I was so angry. Hitting him was the only control I had over the situation at the time.

I did not recognize the power of being absent. I believed that if I had left, Dwayne would have turned his life around. However, I didn't have the confidence to leave him. I had been with him since the 7th grade. I moved from being a dependent of my mother, to being a dependent of his parents. All that I knew about life as an adult, I learned with him. I couldn't fathom the idea of starting over.

I was so afraid to lose him. At one point, Dwayne became the sole breadwinner in our family. He would work all hours of the day, so I would rarely see him. He began taking on regular shifts at his job which meant I needed to stay home with the kids all day.

Even though I was afraid to lose Dwayne, I also felt like I was a prisoner. I felt as if I needed him to make my image of a family complete. I did not want to subject my children to being around any other men. The idea of dating and bringing men home to my children took my mind back to the Monster my mother brought home. How could I trust bringing another man into my children's lives after being raped by the man my mother brought into mine. I had a daughter and was not willing to risk her experiencing the same fate. Dwayne had his problems, but at least I knew my kids were safe with him.

Plus, the last thing I wanted was for God to be mad at me. I remember being taught through religion that God hates divorce. I just wanted to be a good wife and please

God, so for years, I stayed and operated in pure dysfunction.

I had given up my life, my identity and all of my potential. Everything that was me had been reduced to settling for being a man's wife. I couldn't think far enough ahead to see that I could be a wife, have my own opinion independent of my husband's thoughts, and also support my own dreams that I had for my life.

I stayed through all of the pain and deceit. I even participated in the infidelity myself and had an inappropriate extramarital relationship. I figured, *If you can't beat em, join em.* When Dwayne found out about my affair, he became distraught—as if he hadn't participated in such acts himself. He couldn't take the retaliation. It seemed like he would kick up his affairs three notches every time. We were going back and forth hurting one another over and over again. I knew that what I was doing was wrong, and I was tired of fighting fire with fire. Dwayne, on the other hand, kept going on and on with affair after affair—having one woman after the next. This went on for years.

I stood idle in full compliance because I thought that he would see me respecting our union, and his conscience would call him into order. I will admit that Dwayne and I did not have constant turmoil in our relationship. There were intermittent good times for us. When things between him and I were good, they were really good. He showered me with love, gifts, and precious memories. We had inside jokes, I can honestly say that no one else knew me the way that he did.

Although I was unhappy at times, I just held on to the good times in hopes he would come to his senses and see how much I loved him and that I was hurting; but he never did. Dwayne had eventually settled into a relationship with two other women, one was a mutual acquaintance named Maree. Maree was a girl who went to high school with us. I didn't know what he saw in her; she was easy. All the guys from high school and the neighborhood had her; but for some reason, he loved and took care of her as if she were me. When I found out about the way he was carrying on with her, it took a toll on my self-esteem. I started comparing myself to Maree, not knowing that I was special, and his extramarital relationships were a reflection of how he saw himself and had nothing to do with me.

I was going through a broken marriage. I couldn't talk to my mother because she never tried to understand me. We didn't have the type of relationship where I could be raw with emotion. Any time it got too deep, I was always told to pray about it. There I was, going through the toughest time of my life, alone.

I even agreed to compromising the sanctity of our relationship. He proposed that we adopt an "open" relationship. I thought that agreeing to this would save our marriage. I was sorely mistaken. This did absolutely nothing but made everything even more complicated. There was so much confusion and chaos. I knew that I had to stop. Besides it wasn't something that I wanted for myself. It was yet another thing that I had allowed and accepted because I believed that it would make my husband happy.

The relationship between Dwayne and I was so toxic, but I was used to living in a toxic environment. Dwayne even told me that "better didn't exist". I believed him because for my entire life, I had never seen anything different. I knew that things between Dwayne and I were bad, but I never thought that I would literally be putting my life and the life of our children in jeopardy for simply loving him.

A DOUBLE LIFE

One day everything hit the fan! Literally. The chain of events would put my life on a path that would change everything forever. I was at work on a lunch break when I received a phone call from Dwayne. The conversation started out like any of our other conversations would.

"Hello?" I answered.

"Hey, I have something to tell you," he said in a somber tone.

"What's up?" I asked.

"The Feds got me."

I didn't comprehend what he was saying. He didn't sound like he was in any kind of serious trouble, so I had no clue that anything as serious as being arrested was a possibility. Besides, he was a business owner. He owned several businesses. I couldn't wrap my mind around the words I had just heard.

"What are you talking about?" I asked, thinking this was some kind of joke.

"I got arrested," he said, as a matter of fact.

"Arrested for what? What did they say?" I was ready to go fight for my husband. This had to have been a racist attack on a successful Black businessman.

"They got me on conspiracy to distribute."

"Distribute what?" I asked, still not understanding.

"Drugs!" He said impatiently.

"But you're calling me from your cell phone," I said. I was waiting for him to get to the punch line. Instead, he calmly told me that he had, indeed, been arrested by the federal government for selling drugs and that we would talk more when we got home.

I had to finish my work shift in a ball of emotions, fear, and confusion. My husband just called to tell me he was a big time drug dealer and had been arrested by the "feds". Was this a dream? I rushed home to find Dwayne sitting at the dining room table.

"What is going on?" I demanded.

He calmly told me to sit down. What followed was a full confession of a life he was living that sounded more like something out of a movie. He went on to tell me that he and his mistresses, for whom he lost his eyesight, were arrested for drug conspiracy. I was floored. He explained that the cops arrested him, showed him some pictures and then let him leave. I figured that if they let him go, they must not have had a strong case. Perhaps this would blow over quickly, but as time went on, everything came to light.

I later found out that Dwayne was trafficking narcotics with a couple of his family members, a few friends and one of his mistresses. He confessed that he had multiple businesses and homes. I was looking at a complete stranger. This man was my husband, the father of my children, and slept next to me night after night, yet I didn't know who he was.

As he told me more and more about this double life, I lost all respect for him. My husband was a big, tall, husky man-- 6 feet tall, 300 pounds — but the more he spoke, he began to look small and weak to me. At that moment I didn't see a man or my husband, I saw a little boy who had allowed this world to use him like a puppet. We had sons. What kind of an example of a man was he being for them at this point? He had finally done it. He had chartered into unforgivable territory.

Immediately, my mind was open and clear. I began to see him for the man he was all along. I was in love and only wanted to see the best in him, but now I was able to see through the smoke and mirrors. When Dwayne told me to stop smoking weed, it wasn't because he cared about me. It was about controlling me. When he was hanging out with his friends in high school and coming home with wads of money, I gave him the benefit of the doubt, but now I realized that he was not the good old church boy I thought he was.

Then I realized that I had been putting my life in danger all along. According to an article published in *The Science Daily*, a person experiences about four near-death experiences in a lifetime. I have experienced approximately six within the time I met Dwayne all the way to the day we separated.

I remembered when we were seventeen. I was pregnant with my first born. We were driving in his car when someone opened fire on the vehicle striking the rear passenger door as I sat helplessly in the front passenger seat.

This incident could have ended my life and the life of my unborn child. I never assumed it had anything to do with Dwayne.

In an instant, I realized that there had been glaring red flags from the very beginning. I was so captivated with having a family and being in love that I was blind to what was so obvious. I felt so embarrassed. What would my family think? Yet, even with my blinders falling away and my utter disgust with this pathetic excuse of a man sitting in front of me, the empath in me felt sorry for him and wanted to protect him. He needed a lawyer, so we sold everything to scrape together $10,000 for a retainer fee. We couldn't afford the house we lived in any longer therefore I decided that the children and I would relocate to Tennessee.

I wanted to leave him and his double life, but Dwayne played the role of the repentant husband.

"Baby, let's put all of this behind us and start fresh."

Against my better judgment, I decided to give it a try. I remembered the young, well-dressed respectful boy I fell in love with as a kid. Perhaps we could find those kids again in Nashville. I could finally have my husband to myself away from his mistresses, double life, and negative influences. Maybe our marriage had a chance of survival.

We began a life in Tennessee, but it was short lived. After only a few months, Dwayne's pretrial counselor informed him that he was unable to stay in Tennessee because he was fighting a federal case pending in the state of Illinois. Dwayne would travel back and forth to make court dates and check in with his pretrial administrator. While in Chicago, Dwayne was supposed to be living with his mom, but he soon found his way back into the home of one of his other mistresses that was unrelated to the case. While I was in Tennessee struggling to keep things together for our family and working an overnight job, Dwayne was enjoying the single life floating between both mistresses.

Dwayne still had the support of his mistress that was included in the federal indictment. While I was in Tennessee, Dwayne and the second mistress would attend our family church as if they were a couple. They had joined and supported different ministries within the church and were establishing a foundation with the church. I felt like I was losing all over again.

Instead of letting go, I went into fight mode. I uprooted my children and went back to Chicago because I wanted to fight for my marriage. It seems so ridiculous, now that I'm writing these words. I guess it's true what they say: "Hindsight is 20/20." When I moved back to Illinois, I lived with my mother-in-law for a couple of years while Dwayne fought his federal court case.

Dwayne's mother and I had a strained relationship because she supported Dwayne's mistresses. His mother knew about all of them and had relationships with them. She and other members of Dwayne's family also went to several dinner parties and events with the mistresses. I felt as if the entire family had betrayed me. I looked at everyone as an enemy instead of seeing the power that I had in me to change my surroundings.

I came to realize that the entire family was living this double life. Not only was Dwayne this big time Chicago drug dealer, but he was supporting his entire family and all of his mistresses. Everyone seemed to benefit from this alter-ego my husband had except me. While he was making hundreds of thousands of dollars, I was working to pay bills. It was as though Dwayne had put our relationship on some kind of twisted, warped, schizophrenic pedestal.

200 MONTHS

In 2015, our oldest son and I attended the final court date on the federal charges against Dwayne. This was the day of sentencing. Before the verdict, Dwayne requested all of the family members to write letters of character. One of his character witnesses mentioned the fact that Dwayne cheated on me. I know this because the Judge scolded Dwayne when passing down his sentence.

"Your actions have left a scar on the community," the Judge said. "You haven't been the ideal husband by the way you treat your wife and children by being involved with drugs and other women. I know that you have a young family, but you must pay for your actions"

The Judge handed down a 200 month sentence in a federal penitentiary. With the bang of the gavel, Dwayne's double life was over. He lost everything: money, family, wife and children. I was sure that 200 months wasn't that long because God knew that I loved Dwayne and that he wouldn't allow us to be apart that long. God knew how much the kids loved their father, I knew for sure that God would not make me raise my children alone.

My initial reaction was to Google how many years was 200 months. When the search results showed that 200 months is in actuality 16 years, I was completely shocked. My stomach did a million flips and I fainted right out on the courtroom floor. The bailiff ran over to assist me but once I came to, I was inconsolable. I pleaded with the Judge asking him to have mercy as if he was God himself. I had no idea what would become of my children and me. I wasn't used to being on my own for 16 hours in a day, what in the world was I supposed to do without Dewayne for 16 years?

The Judge did not immediately take Dwayne into custody. The courts allowed him to stay out for two years while he recovered from the cornea replacement surgery needed after our encounter with my keys. Hopefully the courts would forget about everything, and Dwayne wouldn't go to jail. Stranger things have happened, and I have seen a miracle or two in my lifetime. I felt like the right thing to do was to endure the pain and fight for the marriage even if I was the only one fighting. Maybe this was some kind of miracle happening? Maybe God was giving me a buffer before my husband had to go away for those 16 years? Maybe there was time for us to salvage the marriage? Maybe my husband would come to himself and realize that I was here for him all along and love me the way that I wanted to be loved? Maybe he would finally forsake his mistresses and cleave to me like the Bible said? All kinds of thoughts ran through my mind.

Time went on, and we tried to go about life as normally as we possibly could. We planned an afternoon outdoors to take family portraits. I wanted my children to have pictures with their father before he was sent to prison for 16 years of their lives. Our youngest child would be 22 years old before we would have this opportunity again, so this was at top priority in my eyes.

It was a fun afternoon and somewhat of an escape from what was happening in life. We took some beautiful family photos to show the world that we were a strong family, but behind the photos was a wife with paper thin patience, a husband with wandering eyes and a few somewhat happy and unsuspecting children.

Every single day after court was a gift in my mind. I knew that at any given day, the federal government was coming to collect. No one knew exactly when. However, it didn't take long for Dwayne to go back to his old ways. Although he was facing 200 months in prison, he was still running the streets with his two women. You would think the idea of losing your freedom would cause you to change your ways and appreciate the blessings God has given you, but he did not.

I made several homicidal threats to kill Dwayne and his mistresses. I tried hitting one of his mistresses with his car. I was willing to do anything to hurt him because I was hurting. These attempts would shift his attention back to me briefly, but he was getting his ego fed by the women who seemed to have been giving him everything I never could.

On several occasions, I planned and attempted suicide by hanging myself. I wrote a note blaming Dwayne for all of my pain so that he would feel guilty for the rest of his life. I knew that he would think of me and weep because of the way he treated me. Fortunately, my attempt to punish my wayward husband by *killing myself* didn't work

The way our bathroom was positioned, the door was right next to the toilet. I stood on the toilet seat, took a thick leather belt, tied it in a loop, put the loop around my neck and with the long piece of the belt I jammed in at the top of the door. I don't remember what was going through my mind at the time, I just felt like this was my only way out. So I stepped off of the toilet and hung there. I don't know how long I was up there before Dwayne burst into the bathroom, and I fell to the floor.

"What are you doing?" He screamed.

"I hate you! I want to see you suffer." I said to him

He looked at me in pure disgust.

"I'm calling the police," he said.

I laid on the floor sobbing, "It's not fair!"

I felt so broken. The only way I felt that I could win was to harm myself. I wanted him to feel the hurt and pain that I was feeling.

The ambulance came, and I was admitted for Psych evaluation. I stayed in the hospital for four days. While I was there, I saw other people who were fighting their own battles and who had attempted suicide. For once, I had thought of my children and how they would feel if I had never come back home, so I vowed to never attempt suicide again for the sake of my children. That alone didn't stop the thoughts of suicide, but, I just carried on with the weight of my pain like a backpack because I knew that my kids needed me.

Dwayne's response was the total opposite of what I wanted.

"If you commit suicide, I'll have Samira raise the kids!"

Samira was the other mistress. This was a blow to my mind. I used to imagine my children being raised by those women and just get sick to my stomach. Dwayne would take my children around these women, and the kids actually liked them. They would come home from Marees's house saying how much fun they had playing with her kids. Dwayne wanted to replace me as their mother even before my death. Dwayne would deny any wrongdoing and would always tell me that the kids were making things up. I was being severely abused emotionally by the man I loved dearly but did not know that I had the power to change my life.

Dwayne had settled comfortably into his life as husband, father and ladies' man. I was in full compliance with his lifestyle because he controlled the money and the wellbeing of our household. Our kids loved Dwayne dearly, and I did not want to destroy what our children saw as the perfect family. I made up a fortress of excuses to stay, and so I lived in that fortress for years--unhappy, depressed and feeling defenseless about everything that was happening in my life.

I had gained over 100 pounds, I felt unattractive and didn't think anyone would want me being so heavy and having 3 children. I had been brainwashed to think that my friends and family hated me and that I was all alone. I felt as if I had nowhere to go, and so I endured the abuse.

EVERYTHING HAS TO CHANGE

I began to notice Dwayne was carrying two cell phones which was strange seeing that he didn't have a job. *Was he selling drugs again?* I wondered. One was a flip phone, and the other was a smart phone. The smart phone didn't have service, but Dwayne always claimed that he was using it for the internet. One day my youngest son was playing with Dwayne's phone which wasn't uncommon. I took the phone from my son and tried going on a website, and Dwayne became highly defensive.

"Give me my phone!" He snapped!

He was clearly overprotective of this phone.

"Why?" I challenged him. "What are you trying to hide?"

"Nothing. Ain't nothing on the phone. Just give it back."

He tried snatching the phone from me.

"It was okay when our son was playing with the phone, but I can't simply use it to go to a website?"

I knew Dwayne was hiding something from me at this point. Dwayne relented at this point and allowed me to look through the phone. I went through the text and phone call history, and there was nothing to be found. Then, I went to the email. Low and behold, there were messages from Samira. He had been using the wifi on the phone to email her through the prison phones. There was also a message where she thanked him for sending her money. I was livid! Here I am trying to be a good wife and Dwayne was still up to his same tricks.

Not long after finding out that Dwayne was still up to his philandering ways, the federal government sent a letter telling him to turn himself in within 72 hours. Call it Karma or God's punishment, but I didn't find it a coincidence. I wonder how life would have been for him had he done right by me.

Ironically, we had no time to prepare for his departure. He had been free so long, it was as if it slipped our minds. We had gotten used to life as it was and took it for granted. Dwayne's mom had to purchase his plane ticket and prepare to send money for Dwayne's books.

The tragic inevitability had become real at this moment. My anxiety levels had gone through the roof. It was like I was preparing for a war, preparing for what I thought would be the hardest battle of my life and had to make it all happen just in time for dinner. I was in a hurry to secure my children and their emotional wellbeing. So before Dwyane's departure, I had to put on a strong front for the family.

I couldn't share with anyone just how broken I really was. I felt like I had to appear strong for the children. I had to pretend that I didn't need financial help or a shoulder to cry on.

At this point in my life, my family was estranged. I hadn't spoken to my mother in months. I felt like my sister and brother wouldn't understand what I was going through. The only people I really cared about were the three lives who depended on me to make sure they had food to eat, a roof over their heads, and clothes on their backs. I was all that they had at this point.

The following day, the kids and I woke up at 5 a.m. It was the day that we drove Dwayne to the airport. He was headed to Florida to turn himself in to the federal government. The ride to the airport was very quiet, and we seemed to have gotten there very quickly. As the car approached the departures terminal, the tears began to stream down my face. I could not believe that I was about to say farewell to the love of my life for the next 16 years.

All of this happened conveniently during the middle of the week so life had to go on. No matter how broken I felt at the time, I still had to go to work. I went into my office with a brave smile as if I didn't just take a piece of my heart out of my chest and leave it at the airport. I was operating in full blown denial. I was still hoping for some type of miracle to happen. This feeling lasted for over a year. I would still talk to Dwayne on the phone and wire him money occasionally just to make sure that he had the things that he needed.

The kids still had to go to school. I noticed a slight change in all of my children once Dwayne was gone. The two younger children threw themselves into their school work and began performing exceptionally well academically. They went from being C-students to A-students.

On the other hand, my oldest son was very disappointed by what his father had done. He was at a point where he could no longer focus on his academics and wanted to drop out of college. He took the situation the hardest out of all the children because he was the eldest and had a very close relationship with his father. He felt betrayed that his father would risk not seeing him graduate college to selling drugs.

I had to talk to my son about forgiveness and that it was important for him to know that the decisions that his father had made were not a reflection of him. I told him to release himself from the hurt feelings that his father caused.

Although Dwayne was locked away in prison, he still tried to control my every move.

"What time are you leaving work? What time will you be at home? Make sure you write me a letter, tonight."

I'm ashamed to say that I would still answer his questions and concede to his expectations of how I was to live my life in his absence. I was so delusional that I was still depending on Dwayne to somehow lead our family from behind prison walls. I had never taken on the role as head of the house and done things for the family without him being present. I felt as if I was a great co-star and supporting cast member of the family but never looked at myself as being capable of leading. In my delusion, I felt as if I needed Dwayne for that.

I was so dependent and accustomed to Dwayne taking care of me, that one day, I left work, walked across the parking lot to my car, opened the passenger-side door, and took a seat waiting for Dwayne to drive off. I sat waiting for a second until it dawned on me:

"Sis there is no one coming to take this wheel. You gotta do the driving yourself from here on out."

It was then and there that I realized I needed to control the steering wheel of my life. It was time for me to wake up and think for myself, to acknowledge my own needs and my own feelings, to consider my own opinion and not the opinions of others. I had to learn how to establish boundaries and protect myself. It was time for me to show myself the unconditional love I gave everyone else.

I started by confronting my battle with depression. I realized that my depression was fueled by fear of the unknown. I had no idea what my life would look like without Dwayne. He was in my life from the time I was 15 years old. We had grown up together. However, I knew that I deserved better than what he had to offer and decided to seek out counseling.

During my counseling sessions, I told the counselor all about my childhood and the sexual abuse I had endured. I started blaming Dwayne for everything that was wrong in my life. I harped and complained session after session on his cheating and how I was emotionally abused in the marriage. One day, I had an epiphany: I was not being forced to stay in these situations. I could have removed myself at any point. I realized that Dwayne never had any power over me. He only had the power that I had given to him.

My next step was to address my health. I went to the doctor's office and did blood work and was told that I had developed type 2 diabetes. Here we go again. I guess it was time for another existential crisis. My mind was completely blown.

How in the hell did I get here? I wondered.

I read that Black women, ages 20 and older, represent 14% of all diabetes cases in the United States. Black women only account for 13% of the total female population in the U.S., which is staggering. I had to take myself and my health seriously.

I began to take control of my overall health and well-being. For years I had battled obesity. I was living an unhealthy lifestyle, drinking large amounts of alcohol, eating late and completely avoiding the gym.

I prayed to God about my health.

"God, show me what to do to be healed of diabetes!" I prayed.

I began to change my habits little by little. I began making small changes in my daily routine. I began going to the gym and developing a workout routine that consisted of extreme cardio. I initiated portion control when I ate and consumed more green vegetables. I was starting to lose weight and feel better about myself.

I no longer could consume large amounts of alcohol because every time I took a drink, I would immediately get throbbing tooth pains. At first I thought it was a fluke, but it literally happened every single time I took a drink. That made me realize that drinking alcohol was no longer for me. I began researching healthy eating habits. Gradually my diet changed completely. Over time, I totally reversed diabetes in my body. I no longer take any medications and walk in 100% health.

For the first time in my life, I guarded my time, my resources, and my entire being. I was at a point where I could no longer give to anyone else because I needed me. I went into full self-preservation mode. I had finally had enough of living my life the way I had been living. *Everything had to change immediately.* I began living life on my terms. I noticed I was waking up anticipating the day. The sun seemed brighter, colors more vibrant—I was experiencing true happiness.

My self-esteem was starting to develop. I had never felt a sense of power in my life before. I started to feel strong because I saw myself changing for the better. I found a new sense of liberation. There were so many goals I had put off in life to concentrate on being a wife and mother, but this was my time to do what I wanted to do for myself.

Then it hit me.

I should go to school. I thought.

No one in my family had finished college. This was more than a notion. Was I ready to take on this challenge? After a few days of prayer, I made up my mind. I was going to do it. I was going to get my college degree. I was going to break the cycles in my family. I enrolled myself in Devry University to study Human Resources Management.

Starting school during a particularly difficult time in my life was not ideal, but I knew that furthering my education would assist me in being gainfully employed. Dwayne was opposed to me going to school because he felt that it was a waste of time and money. However, with him no longer having influence over me, that choice was all mine. A few years later, I received my degree. It was one of the happiest moments of my life. It was one of the biggest accomplishments I had achieved in a while. I was looking forward to the future to see what else I could do being out of Dwayne's shadow.

I didn't have time to celebrate receiving my degree because I was on a mission. I needed to move my life in the right direction, so I stayed in grind mode. I just kept moving forward. Soon after receiving my degree, I landed an amazing job at a local financial institution. Getting a foot in the door with an entry level position was ok for the time being, but I knew I needed to make more money than I was making. I was settling into my new normal which consisted of educating myself and taking care of my own health, wellbeing and the wellbeing of my children. I was finally on the right page with myself.

I had really enjoyed living in Tennessee. I wanted to move back so badly. I could remember my children and I all being happy there. I was literally on a quest to be connected with happiness. I felt like Chicago had taken everything from me. I really wanted a fresh start in life. I began to pray from a place of desperation.

"Lord, please open a door for me to leave Chicago. I have no future here. My kids have no future here. I don't want them to follow in the footsteps of their father. Please God, help me!" I begged.

I wanted out of Chicago and away from my in-laws.

"God, lead me to a safe place where my kids and I will be comfortable!" I prayed.

Prayer and faith without action is worthless, so I began to plan what seemed to be my great escape. I saved every dime that came to me through work and picked up a side hustle helping people to manage their social media presence. I did all that I could think of that was legal that would yield an extra dollar for my relocation. I have always been a hard worker, but I put my grind into overdrive.

God began showing me what to do and with whom to connect to help make my move. I was ready to leave Chicago at a moment's notice as soon as the right opportunity presented itself. A few weeks later, I received a big break. I had applied to about a gazillion jobs in Nashville and to my pleasure, I received a call back asking me for an in person interview at a telecommunications company.

This was a great opportunity for me because I would be interviewing for a leadership role which meant that I would be making a decent amount of money. I was starting to see the light at the end of the tunnel. Several days later, I took a day trip to Nashville for an interview, and the meeting went well. I didn't get an immediate offer, but I was extremely hopeful.

I went back to Chicago and began packing and tossing the things that I wasn't taking with me. A few days later, I received a call from the telecommunications company with an offer to start my new role the following week. I was overjoyed to hear the news about the new role. My freedom was only a week away. The next thing I needed to do was secure an apartment for my children and I to live.

I didn't find a rental property when I had traveled to Nashville a few days prior, so I went online to see if I could find a place. I found an apartment that was about 15 minutes away from my new place of employment. The pictures that were online looked like a nice place, and the reviews of the neighborhood were great. I was so eager to move that I placed a deposit on the rental property before I even had a chance to see it in person. I was literally moving to Nashville with my fingers crossed, hoping I wasn't moving to a dump that looked nice online.

The time had finally come. It was time for my great escape. I didn't tell anyone that I was leaving except my children. No one even knew where I was going. I didn't mention my departure to anyone because I was tired of checking in with people. I wanted to move about on my own terms without asking for permission, and that is what I did.

When I got to Nashville, all that I had were my children, my beat up Chevy, a few articles of clothing and maybe a couple hundred dollars. The rent and utilities for the new apartment were paid, so I was content. I was happy sleeping on the floor because my new place was carpeted and clean.

I was 35 years old, and this was my very first taste of independence. This was a major milestone for me. For once in my life, I physically felt free. Immediately all kinds of gifts started to emerge. I developed a passion for public speaking and became comfortable telling my story. I wanted to empower women so that they wouldn't have to suffer the pain that I endured.

The most interesting reveal was my desire to do standup comedy. I had gone to an open mic show at a local comedy bar. I discovered that I can actually make people laugh. I had no idea that I had this ability. This gift virtually came out of thin air. I joked about my relationship with Dwayne and found a new outlet for healing, as I brought joy and laughter out of my pain.

Although I had moved to a new location and my life was starting anew, I was still legally married to Dwayne. Yet, even after all that I had endured--cheating, lies, endangerment, and abuse--the thought of actually divorcing Dwayne was still horrifying.

While Dwayne played the role of Robin Hood to the streets, he neglected to take care of his own family. That was the part that made me despise him in the beginning. How dare you take care of your side women and leave your wife and kids alone to figure everything out. I was totally disgusted with Dwayne and thought less and less of him.

One night, Dwayne called me from prison. He wanted to talk and reminisce on old times. While Dwayne chattered on and on about the good times we had, I was contemplating the best time to tell him I was filing for divorce. I couldn't take any more of his fakeness, pretending that this was not the marriage from hell. While he jabbered on, I cut him off mid-sentence

"I want a divorce!" I blurted out.

He immediately tried to make me feel guilty for it.

"What are you talking about? After all we've been through? You just wanted to wait until I went to jail to divorce me," He said.

"There is never a right time for things like this, but for me, right now is that time." I responded.

"Why do you want to destroy our family?" He asked.

Dwayne knew just how to get into my head. He knew my emotional triggers even before I did. Dwayne knew how much I loved him, He knew that family was my number one priority and that I would have gone to the end of the earth for my family.

"The family has been broken for years Dwayne!" I yelled. "Don't try to act like we've had the picture-perfect family. This family has always been broken." I retorted.

"Clearly, you've been wanting to tear our family apart all this time. You were just waiting for the right time. Now that I'm in jail, I guess it's easy to put the blame on me, huh?"

His manipulation was enraging me at this point.

"The conversation is over!" I demanded. "There is nothing else for us to talk about." I hung up the phone as he continued to protest. Words cannot express how empowered I felt. I had taken back all of my power. I took a deep breath, releasing the anger he had stirred up, and then a faint smile rose up on my face.

When I hung up the phone, I realized that I did not need permission from Dwayne or anyone else to live my God-given life. I was moving forward with the divorce, no matter what. Dwayne was not my God, although he probably believed he was. I was co-creating my own reality alongside the true and living God.

Although I felt bad for Dwayne being away from the family, I started to look at Dwayne's incarceration as a blessing. I realized, Dwayne was not *entirely* wrong. He was right, I did wait until he was in jail. I did need him to be locked up in order to break free from him. God was freeing me from my captor. I was Dwayne's prisoner-- mind, body, and soul. God knew that I would never have left the marriage had Dwayne been present.

Dwayne was in prison, and there was nothing he could do to physically harm me. I was truly free!

CONFIRMATION

I'll admit. For a moment I was still on the fence, even after telling Dwayne it was over. When I went to sleep that night, his voice echoed in my head like a broken alarm clock I couldn't shut off.

"Why are you trying to destroy our family?"
"Why would you wait until I went to jail?"

Somehow, as crazy as it sounds, I began to second-guess myself.

Were things as bad as I was making them out to be?
Was I being emotional?
What about the kids? Will they resent me?

I clearly knew the answer to these questions, but somehow, things had gotten flipped upside down in my mind. But I knew I was doing the right thing, right?

Things were different this time though. Usually, when Dwayne would play games with my mind, I had no one to call on. This time, it was just me and God. I didn't have Dwayne's family in my ear telling me that I was being selfish and that Dwayne was right. For the first time, I had silence-- A good silence. The kind of silence that God can give—peace and tranquility.

"Pray," I heard in my spirit. "When confusion steps in, the best thing to do is to pray."

I got on my knees and said,

"God, show me that I am making the right decision about divorce. I have always been told that You hate divorce. I don't want to be in the wrong. I don't want to lose Your blessings."

One thing about prayer is that when you pray, God always has a response; and when He responded, it was bold and absolute. He gave me all the confirmation I needed to let me know that I was making the right decision to divorce Dwayne.

A few days after I prayed, I received a letter in the mail from Dwayne. This letter came standard just as all of the rest, but when I opened the letter there was an address label that had mistakenly been left inside of my envelope. This label was addressed to Maree.

This it was, I knew that it was time to let go! And I did just that. I wanted Dwayne to have what he had been fighting for all of these years, his freedom. At that point I realized that Dwayne did not owe me anything. I made it up in my mind that I would detach myself from anything that was rejecting me, and so I was finally ready to walk this journey called life without Dwayne.

Sometimes when we think of a relationship that is meant to be, we automatically assume that it will last forever. Maybe it isn't supposed to last forever. Maybe it's just someone who is in your life to teach you something. Maybe forever is not a person, but the knowledge we gain from the person.

My marriage to Dwayne taught me many valuable life lessons. It taught me to honor my feelings, and it taught me to respect and love myself above all else. The most important lesson that I learned in the relationship was to always allow people to be who they are and know when it's time to move on. I learned to never try to control or convince a person to see my value. That was my job.

When I left Dwayne, I had mixed emotions. On one hand, I was angry because the husband that swore to protect me would be the one who was trying to break my spirit. On the other hand, I was relieved. I could now live my life filled with happiness and do what brought a smile to my face and joy without feeling guilty. I feel like Dwayne's incarceration was the power of God at work coming to rescue me because had things not happened the way they did I may have never gained the strength to leave.

When I left Dwayne, I left for good, but I carried so much emotional baggage when I left. I left my last relationship thinking that I wasn't good enough. At times I felt like I didn't deserve to be happy. I left with the poverty mindset that struggling and barely getting by with the bare minimum was the norm. I left the marriage feeling ugly and that my beauty had left me forever. I thought that no one would want me with three kids. I left the marriage feeling unloved and used. I left an angry bitter woman full of confusion.

I left the relationship feeling like I had been blind, and the sun was finally shining in. How could I have let this go on for so long? I had no clue who I was. I had lost all sense of self in this relationship. I didn't know what the future would hold for me.

I realized that this was the very first time in my life that I was a single adult woman standing on my own two feet without the support of a man or anyone for that matter. I felt liberated as if my life was going to change forever, and that's exactly what happened. This detachment from Dwayne was helping me to see what life was all about. It was about loving myself and others unconditionally and I was all for it.

For over two decades I had relinquished control of my life and my own free will. I had grown accustomed to ONLY being my children's mom and Dwayne's wife. It was as if my identity was erased, and it was up to me to rebuild myself from the ground up.

I slowly had to remember who I was and that I had real friends from whom I distanced myself. I'm sure these friends would have been there to support me if I asked them. I had forgotten that younger girls looked at me as a role model because I seemed to have it all together on the outside. I had colleagues who respected me as a business woman. Most importantly, throughout all of the years that had gone by and the achievements I had made, *I had forgotten me.*

NO MORE CHAOS

When I left Dwayne, I briefly entered into another relationship. I was tired of being lonely and was willing to settle for more chaos. I quickly noticed that I was attracting the same kind of man as Dwayne but in a different body! After that relationship, I had grown frustrated with dating and just gave up to focus on myself. I made it up in my mind that the type of men I would date after I healed would be the polar opposite of what I was accustomed to. I knew that the type of men I would date would not change until I changed myself. I realized that *I had to become the love that I wanted to have in my life.* Attracting my soulmate had absolutely nothing to do with the way other people saw me, but it had everything to do with how I saw myself.

In all honesty, I had lived my entire life dealing with chaos and drama. I had heard about what a normal relationship was supposed to be like, but was never involved in one. It was not until I was forced to discover life God's way. In order to live my best Godly life, I had no other choice but to start with me.

I had to face myself and everything that had happened to me. My mind replayed my entire life and every decision that had led me to the very spot where I was standing. I had to take responsibility for accepting emotional abuse at the hands of someone I trusted to protect me.

I wanted to talk to one of my married friends about what I was going through, but it seemed as if they were far removed and couldn't relate to me. I felt isolated. I didn't know anyone who had experienced divorce. I was completely alienated by my married friends at that point. I felt like I didn't have a place. My married friends had turned their backs on me because I was no longer part of that "tribe". I tried to blend in with my single friends, but I was still emotionally exhausted from my marriage and the short time I spent in the dating world.

My single friends were living their best lives dating, traveling, and having lots of fun. Since I wasn't ready to date again, I figured that I would just stick to what I knew best and that was being a mommy. Besides, my kids had also suffered a huge loss and needed my love and attention.

In my unhealed state, I had formed trauma bonds with several individuals that had contributed to me being spiritually stagnant. The best way to describe trauma bonds are emotions that make you feel closer to your pain and more loyal to people who are entertained by your pain or have experienced similar trauma themselves.

While you are in a trauma bond connection, it appears that the person who relates to you the best is an ally, however these types of individuals are in desperate need of healing themselves but don't realize it. They see your trauma as something worse than what they are experiencing; and so they appoint themselves to you in order to "help", but the toxic connection will only keep you dwelling in your trauma sometimes on a daily or continual basis.

This refers to a state of being emotionally attached not to a kind friend or family member but to an abuser. I had connected with other people and formed loyal bonds with individuals who were in similar situations as I was or who were entertained by my trauma. We would trade stories of our trauma, and as a result were attributing to the trauma to either be relieved or prolonged. There was never a stage of healing that ever took place so the cycles were repeating.

God showed me who those individuals were and allowed me to gracefully exit those relationships. I was determined that I would have no more chaos!

A QUEST FOR GOD

I never knew the true power of God until the age of 33. All my life, I had gone to church regularly, Sunday after Sunday. I had gotten baptized, sang about freedom and forgiveness in the choir, helped those less fortunate than I, and was excited to tell others about the God I served. But, when I went home, I wasn't seeing the God that I sang about. I knew that I had to be doing something wrong, so I went on a quest to seek the true and living God.

If you want to seek God, you must understand one thing. Before you can find Him, He is going to require you to clean yourself up. When Moses walked up to the burning bush, God told him, "Remove your shoes, because the place where you stand is Holy ground." When the priests would go into the Temple, there was a ceremonial cleansing they had to perform. God is Holy, and when you seek Him, you will have to address your dirt.

Yes, I was a victim in some areas, but I was the villain in others. God does not do pity parties. He is a gracious God, and He will wipe your tears of hurt, but with that same love, He will hold you accountable for your own wrong.

If I was going to find God, on my search, I had to face the ugly truth which was my life. The events that I had endured--needed to be unpacked. I remember looking at myself in the mirror as if I had been waiting for *me* to arrive. Everything that I had been through was looking right back at me. I had no other choice but to face it.

When I began the healing process, I felt like a student in a classroom of one. There were no other students that I could talk to who understood what I was experiencing. I couldn't copy anyone's notes. I had to sit with myself and evaluate every single thing that had gone on in my life. I would have to complete this task from the inside out. My personal healing and forgiving others was going to have to start with me. I had to forgive myself. I had to literally take inventory, throw away the things that didn't make sense for me to keep and keep the things that I knew I needed.

The first demon I had to face was unforgiveness.

FORGIVENESS

For years I held unforgiveness in my heart towards my mother. My relationship with her was strained from Tony and her refusal to deal with the aftermath of what he had done to me. I resented her because she brought that monster into our home. I didn't have the courage to sit her down and tell her what I felt. Instead, I would just lash out at her for the slightest misunderstanding, and she never knew why I would blow things out of proportion.

I held on to unforgiveness against Dwayne and his family for all that they had done to me during our relationship. I think I held on to that bitterness with both hands. I hated him for the pain he put me through by cheating on me constantly. I believed that I had a right to my anger and resentment, but in God's eyes, I did not.

God showed me that forgiveness was not for the offender. Forgiveness was for me. God tells us that before we pray, we have to forgive those with whom we have an "aught" (grievance) **before** we can pray to Him. If we don't forgive them, God will not hear our prayers. (Mark 11:25)

I could not find God until I forgave those who had hurt me--including Tony. It may sound strange, but I had to reach back and show love to my inner child, in order to forgive Tony. Forgiving Tony was more about affirming and healing young Tanica than it was about forgiving Tony's actions. Tony did what he did, and it could not be reversed. Perhaps he never felt a day of guilt for what he did, even after he went to prison. I could not change Tony. I could only change me.

I wanted young Tanica to know that she did not deserve what had happened to her and that she was loved. I apologized to my younger self for what happened. This part lasted for months. I would just grieve what happened. I sobbed and cried inconsolably, hugging myself and telling myself how sorry I was that this had happened to me.

Suddenly, my attention had shifted from Tony and the horrible act that he had done to the younger me. I was more concerned with showing young Tanica the love she had missed. I spoke words of affirmation and love over myself

"I love you Tanica!" I repeated over and over.

"I'm sorry this happened to you Tanica!"

I spoke healing words of affirmation over my younger self.

"You are healed, Tanica!"

"You are safe, Tanica!"

"You are loved, Tanica!"

"You are protected, Tanica!"

This positive self-talk to my inner child went on for several days until it was as if little Tanica stood up with a smile on her face, and walked away healed and free from the chains that had kept her bound. For the first time in my life, the dark secret, hurt, and pain that I had carried inside for so long evaporated, and I was whole. Forgiving Tony was an afterthought--a byproduct of what I truly needed. Little Tanica was free.

EGO DEATH

Overcoming my challenges were far from done. Even more difficult than healing from the pain of past hurts is killing the ego. After Dwayne went to jail, I had to sell everything that I had of value. I was very happy with my accomplishments and the facade that I presented to the world. I couldn't tell my friends and family that I was down to nothing. It was already embarrassing enough to be the laughing stock among friends. I couldn't bear it. So I hid my losses from the world. I took my L's in private while smiling on the outside and just kept on living through the loss of my pride and worldly possessions.

The losses that I had to endure were enough to pierce the soul. I didn't have a shoulder to cry on because there was nobody left. There was either a total falling out of the friendship that made it unsalvageable, death, distance, you name it. It was scary! God separated me and put me in a place where it was only me and Him. God wanted me to realize that the things that I had accumulated were things that could be replaced.

He wanted me to have something that I had never possessed before and that was my sense of self. He wanted me to see who I was on the inside. God wanted me to see myself without the house, the cars and the money. He wanted me to be myself, not the business owner and social butterfly. God was not concerned with preserving my image to the outside world. He had allowed this to happen for my good.

I even lost my car. My car was totaled, and I had to be reminded of what it felt like to ride the city bus back and forth to work. He wanted to see if I would complain since I was working a job that barely provided for my basic living needs. He really broke my pride.

God wanted me to grow in humility and show gratitude even if I didn't have the latest trends in fashion. He wanted me to seek Him with all my heart, with or without possession. I learned to understand what Paul meant when he said, "I know how to be abased and I know how to abound." (Philippians 4:12) God allowed those things because He wanted to bless me with better. He is strengthening me to be faithful with little, and I hold fast to the day when He will proclaim, "Well done, good and faithful servant; **you** have been **faithful over a few things, I** will make **you** ruler **over** many **things**. Enter into the joy of your lord."(Matthew 25:23)

Once God revealed to me that there were greater things that I had been called to in this life, I still struggled to let go of my once thriving business. I had opened three retail storefront shoe stores. My flagship store front was inside of the largest mall in Illinois. The second storefront was located on the south side of Chicago and another on the Westside of Chicago.

The name, Footworks Shoetique, was beginning to become a household name in the city. People would travel far and wide just to support. My company had accounts with some of the most sought after brands. My business also had affiliations with stars from *The Real Housewives of Atlanta*, *Basketball Wives*, and *Love and Hip Hop*. I was so happy about all the momentum that was building surrounding the company and at the possibilities of where we could go.

I kept the business afloat knowing that I was supposed to close temporarily. I needed time to figure out this new me that was trying to emerge. At the same time, I was fearful of what people would say about me closing the business. I assumed that everyone would think I was broke. I had made up all of these scenarios of how people would judge me and laugh at me for being a failure in business. I kept buying inventory and was barely selling any of it. I was accumulating debt just to save my image.

It took me three years to bring myself to terms with what needed to be done. I was holding on to my business with both hands, pleading, "anything but this God!" But I finally released it.

I made the big announcement over my social media platform to over 50,000 followers,

"With a clear heart, we humbly announce that after 15 years in business, Footworks Shoetique is closing. We thank you for your business over the years and appreciate all of the support. We will be rebranding all of our social media pages to reflect the new direction that we are headed in at a later date. Thank you so much for being the best part of Footworks."

ACCEPTANCE

Lastly, God brought me to a place of acceptance. In this moment, I knew I had to stop blaming my Mother, Dwayne and anyone else for how crappy things looked in my life. I had to accept the fact that I was not a victim of my circumstances and that I was indeed a good person, not the things that happened to me over time.

Once I accepted my true self, I accepted my flaws, quirks and all that makes me who I am. Soon after, those parts of me that were once hidden began to resurface, except they weren't exactly the same. They were an even *better version of me--* a more mature, sound version. It seemed like I had been given the gift of life all over again. It felt like a rebirth.

During my rebirth process, I had to isolate myself so that I could really hear what God wanted to say to me. I felt like I was a caterpillar going through metamorphosis. There were plenty of nights that I sat on the side of my bed crying out to God asking for help, asking for the Lord to take the pain of betrayal and the hate that I had in my heart.

I was in my cocoon, and there I dealt with everything. I began to journal on my life and all that happened--good or bad. I started to remember things that I had forgotten, suppressed memories that were hidden, acknowledging every event, forgiving people that had wronged me, and releasing myself from every offense.

This process took over nine months. There were no friends or family to assist me through this process; *it was just me and God.* When I emerged from my cocoon. I was a new creature like the monarch butterfly, the most beautiful one of all. I was completely changed. I didn't sound the same. My woe-is-me sob story had ceased. I was speaking from a place of empowerment instead of defeat. The life that I had lived before today no longer had a negative effect on me.

God made me realize that there was so much power in letting go. I was holding to this life of defeat and heartbreak out of fear. I wanted better, but was afraid to leave things, people and situations that were no longer of service to my greatest good.

I thank God for rescuing me from my own personal hell. If the chain of events hadn't occurred the way that they did, I would not be who I am today.

LOVE ME, FIRST!

When I began to do what was right for me, I was freed from the expectations and opinions of others. For so long, I wanted everyone around me to be happy, and I compromised my own happiness. It took a lot of growth to realize that I was not responsible for how other people felt. It was like a weight had been lifted off of my shoulders. When I announced my business was closing, it was like I was telling the world that I was living life my way no matter what anyone thought.

I had to make amends with myself for neglecting my feelings and needs for the sake of others. I had put myself last for over two decades. I had allowed everything else to run my life. I allowed other people's opinions of me to dictate what I accomplished in life. I wasn't even Tanica anymore, I felt like a shell of the person.

I had arrived at a point where I accepted that everything was not okay, but all would be well. I no longer had to pretend that I wasn't angry and bitter about the circumstances that I had experienced in life. For the first time in a long time, I wanted to be free. I wanted to feel better. I wanted to experience what true happiness felt like and live there, even if it was just a little while-- I take that back, I wanted to live there forever.

I started to learn more and more about myself and Self-love through meditation, books and music. I began to see that Self-love motivated me to make healthier choices. I began to hold myself in high esteem. It helped me nurture my well-being and serve myself before others.

Self-love was foreign in the beginning. At first, I felt a bit guilty because *Self-love* sounded very selfish. I was always taught to love everything and everybody before myself. I had no idea that Self-love was a thing. When I first heard about Self-love, I immediately associated that with arrogance. It was frightening. I was afraid of what people would think of me if I were to ever utter the words *"I love myself"* in public. I was afraid that I would be looked at as being an ungodly person-- not as a multifaceted being capable of loving myself and others.

Too many people feel that modesty is a virtue, and while this is somewhat true, for me, loving yourself is completely different from arrogance. Loving yourself is a solid foundation to which the rest of your beauty comes to the forefront. You must support yourself against the weight and struggles of life.

You cannot truly stand in the world unless you can stand behind yourself, and the only way to do that is to have a solid foundation of Self-love upon which your life can grow and flourish. If you are building a life that is not fortified with Self-love, then your building will not stand. You cannot build on principles you do not have. This goes for relationships, careers, and your personal goals.

You cannot offer another person real love if you cannot offer it to yourself first. You must love yourself for the beautifully flawed person you are.

As God began leading me through this journey of Self-love, He revealed to me that it has nothing to do with being an arrogant person, but everything to do with self-confidence, self-respect, self-esteem, and most importantly loving the God in me. How can you say you love God and not love His creation? How can you love God and not love yourself?

I was finally here! This was the year that God stepped in and completely renewed my mind. I had been doing this work on my mindset on a daily basis. I made sure that I was acknowledging the things that I loved about myself, being appreciative of the things that I had, loving on my children more, and just being present in my own life.

Once I began living in this mindset on a daily basis, my search was complete. God began to show Himself to me. He began speaking to me regularly, giving me insight on where He was taking me in life. This is when He revealed to me that I was writing this book.

It was an early, brisk morning. As I lay in bed, the sun slightly peeked through the mini blinds. The birds chirping outside of my window. It was tranquil and serene. I lie there, warm and cozy, enjoying the moment. Suddenly, God spoke to me in a loud voice,

"Love is the answer."

I sat up, confused about what I had just heard. It didn't make any sense to me.

It can't be that simple! I thought to myself.

"Love? That's it?" I asked.

"If you love yourself the way that I love you, that is when everything changes." God confirmed.

I searched for my phone and opened the Bible app. I was looking for something that I had heard in church plenty of times but this time it finally made sense. *1 Peter 4:8 "Above all, show deep love for each other, for love covers a multitude of sins."*

When I began to love myself and others without judgment, accepting people for who they are completely, that love began to transmute any and all negativity that tried to attach itself to me from that day forward. It was amazing how God showed me this. Life became a bit simpler once I adopted this concept. I was excited to share what I had learned with anyone I came in contact with.

Nobody is perfect, but if you love yourself in your imperfection, you will enjoy an amazing life. Self-love is something I have toiled with a lot over the past few years. Sadly, I, like many people, had never worked on any foundation of Self-love.

Your building may be standing 20, 30 or even 50 plus years, but that doesn't mean you can't get back to the ground level and begin creating a solid foundation. If you can love yourself unconditionally, you will be surprised how positively this can affect your life. When you love someone truly, you want the best for them, you will sacrifice, work hard, and give your all to ensure they succeed; but what if that person was you? If that were the case, there is no telling what you could achieve!

So, get back to the ground work. Start at the base, and let the rest wait. Focus on you, be protective of your time and energy. Invest in yourself and your relationship with God. The people in your life may need to adjust to you taking your own time and space, however, it is always necessary to stay grounded and focused on your own tasks, your own life and your own goals.

This is exactly what I have sought to do throughout the rest of my life. I still have a lot of groundwork to do. My foundations are stronger than ever before. After several years, I can finally say, I love myself for the perfectly flawed person I am. I urge you all to love yourself the same.

FREEDOM

I have fought hard for the changes in my life because I want to be free. I want to live my life free from the opinions of other people. I wanted freedom from fear. I wanted freedom from past situations and relationships that led me away from God and who I was. I wanted freedom from anger and resentment.

That's right! Many people think they are punishing their offenders by holding on to anger and resentment, but they are only imprisoning themselves. The person you are angry with is living their life unaware of your anger, while your body grows sick from the stress. Free yourself!

I craved the freedom I am enjoying now. I worked hard for it. I can honestly say, I drew blood, sweat and tears for my freedom. I was on a mission to see this beautiful life that God had promised me here on earth-- not in the sweet by-and-by. I was determined to LIVE my life and not just exist.

God had personally breathed the breath of life back into me. Everything had changed yet, I was more me than I had ever been. I started to appreciate things like the birds singing. I appreciated the green carpet that God had laid out for us to enjoy through trees and nature, and the sun that gave me vitamin D as it shined down on me.

I was free to be myself. I began to stand firm on my belief not to sacrifice my needs for the needs of others who could help themselves. I was free to say no to things that I did not want or have time to do.

I also learned to give people their freedom. I gave people freedom to get upset with me because I didn't want to follow their suggestions for my life. I gave people the freedom to judge me when I don't conform to their demands. I gave people the freedom to gossip about me. I gave people the freedom to be petty and childish, and most importantly, I gave people the freedom to walk away.

I was learning how to walk on my own and pay close attention to my emotions and my spiritual needs. I also began to pay close attention to the people that God *allowed* me to interact with. I learned that there was purpose in every path I crossed and that I should take time to hear what other people had to say, listen objectively without adopting their views. I learned how to observe without absorbing.

I could see that the freedom I was enjoying was transferring over to my children. They saw the changes that I was making and how intentional I was being with my own decisions about life. The greatest gift I have given my children is my personal healing and development. This makes me so happy to say because I honestly didn't think I would get to this point in life.

MIRACLES

The power of God began to show up in ways I had never experienced before. I began to experience miracles in my life. God's healing power began to manifest in my body. I had experienced health issues in the past and had seen subtle changes but what happened for me after my quest for God had great significance. There was simply no other way to explain it except to call it what it was--a miracle.

For a while I had developed severe migraines. The migraines were debilitating. There were times I was behind the wheel of my car, and the migraine would hit. It was so bad that I would have to pull over. Sometimes, I would have to drive with sunglasses at night. The migraines were also accompanied by phantom smells. I would randomly smell sulfur or cigarette smoke. I could not stand the light or sound. Cold air and hot air all agitated the migraines. I just wanted to be in a soundproof, air tight, dark bubble by myself.

I needed to know what was causing this horrible pain, so I went to a specialist for an MRI. After my MRI was complete, the specialist couldn't provide me with a straight answer. She told me that the doctor would read the results of the x-ray to me. "We've taken a look over your x-ray, and have found a small tumor on the left side of your brain," The doctor said. "The tumor is just beneath your skull at the front of your forehead"

"Are you serious?" I replied.

The doctor looked at me with empathy in his eyes. No, this was not happening. I refused to accept it. I had come too far and fought too hard for a better life to lose it.

"I hear what you're saying doc, but this does not belong to me." I informed him.

He looked at me with shock. He realized I was not taking his words as truth.

I left the specialist with more questions than I had before the initial visit. I scheduled an appointment to go back to the hospital for a follow-up visit. The specialist recommended that I have an MRI and CT Scan performed.

Yeah, you need to look again, I thought to myself.

When I left the doctor's office, I was completely devastated. How could I have a tumor on my brain? I was so young. I had children to raise. This couldn't possibly be the way I was going out! Was this a result of all the years of worry, heartache and anger? Lord, had I worried myself to an early grave?

On the drive home from my appointment, the scripture came to my mind,

"And these signs will follow those who believe: In My name they will cast out demons; they will speak with new tongues; they will take up serpents; and if they drink anything deadly, it will by no means hurt them; they will lay hands on the sick, and they will recover." (Mark 16:17-18)

So, I did just that. I laid my hands on the left side of my forehead.

"I am healed!" I yelled into the air. "I am healed. You said I can lay hands on myself and I shall recover. This does not belong to me. I am healed in Jesus' name."

I believed that I was healed as definitively as I believed I was driving home. I moved on with my day as if I hadn't received any disturbing news. I did go home to my children to let them know what happened at the specialist. I wasn't going to lie to them, but I also didn't want them to worry about me. They had enough happening with their father being incarcerated.

When I got home from my visit to the specialist, I sat my children down and put on a brave face.

"First off, no matter what, everything was going to be fine. I just came from the specialist ,and they said I have a tumor on my brain." I said.

"You're going to be fine," my daughter said, and went back to what she was doing. My youngest son didn't have a reaction at all.

I was happy because they had lined up in agreement with me for my healing.

A week had gone by, and it was time for my second appointment with the specialist. I was nervous yet hopeful. I went to the receptionist to check in for my procedure.

"Good Morning, I'm Here for a CT Scan and MRI."

"What is your last name?" The receptionist asked.

"Jackson," I replied.

"We have been expecting you. The specialist is ready to see you now," She said.

I went into a room anxiously waiting for the specialist to walk in. When she came into the room she greeted me.

"Good Morning Ms. Jackson. I see we will be doing a CT Scan and MRI for you today.

I am ready to order the procedure right now, but we will have to cut out a few of your braids." she said.

"Cut my braids? Nah. I'll just have to come back in a month. I just got my hair braided," I said.

The specialist scheduled a third appointment for the additional tests, and I made my way back home.

A few weeks later, I went on to have the additional tests done. I continued to speak to God, saying this is not my tumor. Once the last test was done, the doctors called me in to read the results of the exam.

"I took a look at the results of your exam and didn't see any activity," The Doctor said.

"So is the tumor still there?"

"Yes it's still there, but it hasn't grown or changed form since your last visit. The growth is not a concern."

"So the tumor died?" I asked.

"Yes the tumor is dormant and won't affect you. How are the migraines?" He inquired.

"I haven't had a migraine in a while. It's been a few weeks." I replied.

The migraines had stopped completely, and I never took the migraine medication ever again. I just accepted the fact that God had healed me and began to walk in my healing. It was one of the most amazing feelings that I had ever had. I praised God because I knew that a miracle had taken place. I was completely healed.

RECONCILIATION

One morning as I was waking up, the Spirit of the Lord spoke to me and said,

"Go Home and clean up."

I was confused because I was already at home, and my apartment was spick and span.

"I'm already home God, where do you want me to go?" I replied.

"Go to your Mother."

"God, I just quit my job. How can I travel to Chicago right now? I don't have the money to go!" I replied.

"I will give you the *wherewithal* to do what needs to be done. Don't take no for an answer," He said.

I wasn't expecting to receive my last paycheck from my job for another two weeks. Where would the money come from?

The following morning I checked my bank account and low and behold my paycheck had come two weeks early. This was when I knew that God meant business. I immediately paid my rent and made my travel plans. I wanted to see my mom before the year ended, so I planned to travel the day after Christmas.

Although my mother and I had a strained relationship for many years, my heart began to change as I healed. I realized that we are all living our own journey, we are all growing, and learning at our own pace. All humans have challenges that we have to face as individuals. Mothers are not superheroes, no matter how much we would like them to be. They have their own broken and unhealed little inner children. They have pains, insecurities and weaknesses. They too will make mistakes.

My mom was young when we experienced those harrowing times together. We literally grew up together. I began to focus on the good that my mother did instead of the mistakes. Although she was dealing with challenges of her own, she made sure that my siblings and I stayed together. She kept a roof over our heads and food on the table. My siblings and I turned out just fine, and I have my mother to thank for that. I was ready to forgive my mother.

The trip to my mother's home was nerve wracking. I usually drive fast, but I was obeying every speed limit to the digit--if the speed limit was 40, I was going 39.5.

I had finally arrived at my mother's house, put the car in park, and sat for a moment to compose myself.

Lord, what am I doing?

I was so nervous. I hadn't been alone with my mom in years. I would usually visit with the kids, and they would be a buffer between my mother and I. My legs felt numb when I decided to step out of the car. Maybe it was due to the freezing Chicago winter air. As soon as I stepped out of the car, my lips dried up. I forced myself up and shut the door slowly. I took a deep breath and forced my fear to the ground.

"I'm not a child anymore. I'm a grown woman. If she forgives me or not, I'm going to let her know that I forgive her," I told myself.

I walked up to the door and rang the doorbell. I shivered at the back doorstep waiting for her to answer. I didn't wait long before my mom opened the door and greeted me with open arms. Although it was freezing outside, my mother's warm embrace melted all of the fear away. It was the just warmth I needed.

"Hey Mommy, It's good to see you," I said. I held her tight. I was making up for 20 years of missed hugs all in that moment.

"It's good to see you too baby," as she led me into the house.

"I have some leftovers from Christmas. Are you hungry?" she asked.

"Yes, please. I haven't had your cooking in a long time!" I exclaimed

I was so happy to be at my mother's house-- just me. No kids. Just me and mommy. I honestly felt like an only child. My Mom and I sat for hours, and then the conversation began to deepen.

"Mommy, I know that you were dealing with your own challenges while we were kids," I said. "I just want you to know that you did an amazing job. We all turned out fine," I said.

A look of shock came over her face. She looked at me for a moment silently. I broke the silence.

"You're the bomb!" I said with a smile.

We both began to laugh. Peace and love filled the room. It was as if the resentment, anger, hurt and pain never existed. I was looking at my Shero again; my idol, my Mommy.

We talked about how she used to drink a lot when we were younger. She told me about how she began to seek help for alcoholism.

"I am 10 Years sober," she said.

"Wow mommy! I am so proud of you. We've come a long way." I said. I paused a second and took another bite of my mother's amazing turkey and dressing. I was amazed at how good it tasted.

"We actually grew up together," I said.

"I know," she replied.

"I just want you to know that I love you and that I'm proud of you." My heart was full.

"I love you too baby. I'm proud of you. I raised a prophet," she said.

I could tell that she was relieved. I could also tell that she was happy to see the glimmer of light that now shines on our relationship with one another. I am looking forward to growing with my mother and getting to know her as the woman she is today. She is a better woman for herself and her grandchildren. By the end of my visit, my mom and I had formed a bond that I had longed for my entire life. We both agreed that we needed that visit. Things are looking up for my mother and I.

THE GOLDEN VEIL

I had the most amazing spiritual encounter with God during the COVID-19 Pandemic. The month started out just like all of the other ones before it. I sat down at my desk and wrote out my intentions for the month. That week, I had a brief conversation with the First Lady at my church. She asked me to give a word for the Women's Day Service. When she asked me, I had no idea what I would be speaking on, but I agreed to speak anyway.

There was nothing that could have prepared me for what would be coming my way. I was about to have a story to tell that would have a jaw-dropping response of biblical proportions. I usually partake in intermittent fasting on a daily basis. I fast for 16 hours a day and give myself an 8 hour window to eat my meals. However, God called me to a different type of fast. It wasn't something that I had planned, it sort of just happened.

The fast that I was called to was a 23-hour fast, and I was given one hour to eat one balanced meal for the entire day. During the first week of my aggressive fast, I started to feel a bit under the weather. I really didn't pay it too much attention because I was usually in the house, and it couldn't possibly be the corona virus that had swept the nation.

During this time, I would usually stay in the house and make the occasional store run. I simply chopped it up as allergies or a minor cold. By the end of the first week of my fast, I had experienced symptoms of hot and cold flashes, body aches, fatigue, change in taste, and coughing. I simply thought it was a cold because I hadn't educated myself on the different symptoms of the virus.

In the first week of my fast, I went to the store to get cold medicine and then came back home. I conducted myself in a normal fashion all that week being a mom and host to a friend of mine who had come to visit me from out of town. I cooked dinner for us all because I didn't think there was anything wrong. My condition seemed to have gotten worse, so I decided to quarantine myself. This way, I wouldn't get anyone else sick. Praise God, neither my friend nor my children were affected.

The following day, I received a phone call from my best friend who is a nurse. I told her that I was experiencing cold and flu symptoms, and she immediately recommended that I get tested for the coronavirus. I told her that I did not think I should get the coronavirus test because I don't go outdoors. I went on to tell her that I had gone to the store for cold and flu medicine and that it had been working just fine.

She insisted that I get the test to be on the safe side, so I scheduled a drive-up appointment with the local urgent care facility. Later that day, I heard from another friend, and I also told her that I was feeling under the weather. I shared my symptoms, and she told me that the pain in my chest could be mucus on the lungs and instructed me to go to my local herb store and pick up his herb called Mullein.

I was able to steep the herb as tea or smoke it to get smoke on my lungs. I decided to do both. About two days later, my chest pains had dissipated. While I was in my bedroom isolated from my children, I couldn't eat much. I was still fasting for 23 hours a day.

During this time, I was only able to drink water during my one-hour window that I had set aside along with chocolate ice cream and chocolate cupcakes. It was the only thing I was able to taste. The other thing that I did was dance, sing, and give God praise. Not only did I sing and dance to gospel music, I sang and danced to music that felt good to my soul.

I gave gratitude to God for allowing me to overcome the virus. I spoke words of affirmation over myself saying things like "I have work to do on the earth. I'm supposed to be here. I am healed and no weapon formed against me shall prosper." That went on for about a week. I had felt gratitude for my life that I had never felt before. In hindsight, my diet consisted of foods that would typically be eaten at a birthday party, and with all the singing and dancing I did, one could say that I celebrated my new life while recovering from the coronavirus.

Once the symptoms had subsided, I was given a few days to rest. I was able to eat small portions of food again, and I felt like things were going back to normal. Then came Yom Kippur 2020. Yom Kippur is the holiest day of the Jewish year. Yom Kippur means "day of atonement." It takes place on the 10th day of Tishrei, the seventh month of the lunisolar Hebrew calendar.

According to tradition, it is on Yom Kippur that God decides each person's fate, so Jews are encouraged to make amends and ask forgiveness for sins committed during the past year. The holiday is observed with a 24-hour fast and a special religious service. As I sit here writing this in hindsight, I am astonished because this was everything that I had naturally been doing while I was going through my ordeal recovering from the coronavirus (fasting, worshiping, and praising God).

One night, I was laying on my bed. I laid on my back as usual, but when I opened my eyes, I was in a completely different place. I wasn't afraid because this place felt familiar. I had never seen it before but I remember reading about this place in the Bible. The scripture is found in Numbers 7, and so I could only imagine that it was an actual place. Some versions of the Bible call it the "tent of meeting". Some call it going "beyond the veil". I have heard it called the "secret place", but I refer to it as the "Holy of Holies". Out of nowhere, suddenly I stood in front of a golden veil. It wasn't like the regular gold found here on earth, it was much more vibrant and seemed like it was a living thing.

The veil of the Temple was woven from blue, purple, crimson and white thread, and embroidered with cherubim. The cherubim are a winged angelic being described in biblical tradition as attending to God.

I didn't stand at the veil alone. God was in front of me. He was the one who led me in. I'm saying He, but I did not see the face. The physical form had a build of a very tall man about 10 feet tall. The being was very gentle and kind. He opened the veil on the left side, and we both went in. Once inside, I took a brief look around. The space wasn't very big, but it was very comfortable.

The ceiling looked like living clouds. The space wasn't very well lit but there was enough light for me to see. God and I sat down. I felt God's presence on both sides of me. When God spoke, I couldn't tell if it was a male or female voice. The best I can describe it was an ever-present voice.

God proceeded to tell me,

"I want to use you."

"But, God I'm divorced. I curse sometimes, and I eat weed snacks. How could you use someone like me?" I asked.

God responded to me with Scripture.

"I know every hair on your head." (*Luke 12:7*) "Before I formed you in the womb, I knew you, before you were born I set you apart." (*Jeremiah 1:5*)

I was in complete and utter shock. Was this really happening? God was speaking to me. This was not a dream, but a real one-on-one encounter with God, and I was able to remember every single detail.

I immediately gave God my yes. Once I gave God my yes, He gave me my assignment.

"I will take you from the work of man to do my work." He said.

He called me "a prophet, priest."

"I appointed you as a prophet to the nations." He said. (Jeremiah 1:5)

"I will make your name great in the earth. You are a descendant of The house of David."

"But how God, I only speak English, how will I speak to nations?" I asked.

"You will speak their Language" He said.

I grew concerned that I would fail.

"Don't be afraid of them for I am with you." He said. (Jeremiah 1:8)

He went on to say that I would be the example.

"People serve me with their lips, but do not believe in my power."

At this point, I was shocked to hear all of this. God wants me to show people how to get to and live in His presence.

"When you speak in my name, only say what I give you to say. Do not add anything to it or take anything away from it" He said. (Deuteronomy 4:2)

"If any place will not welcome you or listen to you, leave that place and shake the dust off of your feet as a testimony against them." He said. (Matthew 10:14)

Everything that God said to me was found in the Holy Word. This was how I knew for a fact that I was receiving instruction from the true and living God.

When He spoke, His words were consistent with what I have read before. God never spoke anything outside of His word.

In a flash, I was back in my room. The presence of God was still speaking to me. He told me that he was imparting ancient wisdom into my mind. It was like a three-day download. It felt like I had a slight headache. God started to tell me who to call or text, and I began to prophesy to those for whom God had given me a word.

I was in awe of the encounter. I kept saying,

"Wow! Wow! I am honored that you would use someone like me."

The Holy Spirit stayed with me for several days after My Grand Awakening revealing to me why my marriage didn't work out. It was not God's perfect will for my life, but He permitted the marriage because I wanted it so badly. I kicked and screamed for it. This was why there was so much pain involved in the union. He also revealed to me why my relationship was the way it was between my mother, family and I.

He told me that I was set apart, and I wasn't supposed to be like anyone in my family. He told me that I was different. Everything that had happened in my life suddenly made all the sense in the world. God reminded me that although I had gone through some very tough times, He was right there the whole time. Over the time that the Holy Spirit visited with me, I knew what it felt like to be loved unconditionally.

I rushed to tell my daughter about the encounter word for word. After I finished telling her what had happened my following question to her was

"Do you think I'm crazy?"

"No," she said.

That was good enough for me. I knew at that point that all of the self work had paid off for me. I had to clean up my spirit so that God could have a clear canvas to work with.

I will be the first to admit, my journey hasn't been easy. It has been filled with highs and lows but one thing that I am certain of is that in the end, everything will be worth it. The exciting thing of it all is that this is just the beginning.

***

I was seven years old when a question came to my mind that would nag me for years. I was watching Saturday morning cartoons when the question arose out of thin air.

Who am I? What is my purpose? I asked myself.

I had finally found my purpose. I have received my life assignment. I have many things to do for God, but the greatest of these is Love...

~~THE END~~

The New Beginning.

AFTERWORD

Before I end this book, I want to leave you with a few tools that I believe would be most helpful. These are positive words of affirmations and other techniques that I have used to achieve the joy, peace and Self-love I am experiencing today.

The first thing is a pledge. We usually hear about pledges when we are promising a donation to a worthy cause or pledging our allegiance to our country, but this one is different; it is a pledge of allegiance to yourself. Remember that you are yours before you are anyone else's.

The next thing is a list of positive affirmations that you can use daily to refocus your attention and build upon something you love about yourself. Find time every single day to affirm yourself, and don't wait for anyone or anything outside of you to speak life and light into you. I am a firm believer that if you love yourself first, that love will act as a light to draw more love towards you. So remember, be the Light.

THE PLEDGE

Personal pledge to myself.

I, _____ pledge allegiance to myself. I pledge to love myself unconditionally and to always be kind to myself.

I pledge to be so secure with myself that I will remain in total harmony no matter who I allow to enter or exit my life.

I pledge to be honest with myself at ALL TIMES and be strong enough to remove myself from situations or people who do not serve my greatest good.

I pledge to affirm myself, speak and think highly of myself on a daily basis so that no matter what is said about me, I do not allow it to define my true being.

I pledge to never give up trying and doing what I love.

I pledge to feed myself with knowledge so that I will remain in a continuous state of growth and development.

I pledge to never compare myself to anyone because I have no competition.

I pledge to never pretend to be something I am not.

I pledge to treat myself with respect and never settle for less than I deserve.

CLOSING PRAYER:

My prayer is that this book has inspired you to look within to seek the God in you. I pray that you are enlightened and that this book helps you to know that you too have an assignment and that you should boldly seek after it. I pray that my stories have inspired you to stand in your God given power that you received from birth. And that it gives you the strength to push forward during the tough times and wisdom to fully appreciate the good times. I pray that you have the courage to detach yourself from any and all things that have tried to stunt your growth or have kept you away from seeing your self worth. I pray that you find love and happiness within yourself while you're on your unending journey. Amen.

HEALING AFFIRMATIONS

- I give myself permission to heal.
- I am willing to forgive myself.
- I am ready to forgive anyone I feel has hurt me.
- I let go of my perceived pain.
- I'm willing to see things differently.
- I let go of my need to be right.
- I accept the lesson my pain is offering me.
- I see my current circumstances as an opportunity to grow.
- I allow myself to give and receive love.
- I release the past and trust that everything is happening for my greatest good.
- I take responsibility for the quality of my relationships.
- I am willing to give the love I expect from others.
- I am happy to give without expectations.
- I am capable of unconditional love.
- I treat the people in my life with compassion and understanding.
- I know these circumstances are a gift to help me grow.
- I set myself and others free by choosing to forgive.
- Everything I am going through is making me a stronger, wiser, and more compassionate person.
- I trust that everything in my life is unfolding perfectly.

- I create loving and healthy relationships.
- I am willing to be at peace with myself and everyone.
- I bless the past and embrace the present moment with an open heart.
- I choose to forgive because it feels better to love.
- I accept my part in everything that happens in my life.
- I am willing to amend my own behavior.
- I acknowledge my unresolved feelings with patience and self-reflection.
- I respect and validate the feelings of others.
- I allow the perspective of others to deepen my understanding and love for them.
- I am kind to myself and others.
- I always choose love.

AFFIRMATIONS FOR SELF WORTH

- I deserve to be happy.
- I am worthy of love and attention.
- I deserve success and wealth.
- Believing in myself comes naturally to me.
- I have unique abilities.
- I am worthy of having great relationships.
- Every day my self worth is growing.
- I am attracting good things in my life.
- I am a special person. There's nobody else like me.
- I love myself.
- I am a unique unrepeatable expression of God.
- I love myself more and more each day.
- I am worthy of love.
- I am worthy of happiness.
- I am worthy of success.
- I deserve to be paid well for my skills.
- I am supported in all I do in life.
- I am aware of my gift to the world and share it freely.
- I am compassionate with others and myself.
- I am a positive being, aware of my potential.
- There are no blocks I cannot overcome.
- I love to meet other people and make new friends.
- I am a good person.
- I am confident and strong.
- I am very secure with myself.
- I have very high self-esteem.

- I value and honor my boundaries.
- My self-esteem is growing day by day.
- I believe in myself.
- I believe in my abilities.
- I am in control of my life.
- I am happy and full of joy.
- I am creating a beautiful life.

AFFIRMATIONS FOR SELF-RESPECT

- My friends and family respect me.
- I respect my boundaries.
- I am respected by people around me.
- I am worthy of respect and appreciation.
- I deserve to be treated with respect.
- I attract only people who respect me.
- I love and respect myself for who I am.
- My co-workers appreciate the work I do.
- My relationship is filled with love, respect and trust
- I am recognized, respected and appreciated for my achievements
- I am always worthy of genuine respect.
- I respect other people's values and opinions
- Other people respect me because I respect myself.
- I treat others with respect and interest. I smile and look at them while they talk and show genuine interest in their ideas.

- I focus on the people in my life who treat me well
- I accept and respect other people's values and opinions, and they respect mine
- I am respected by those with whom I work.
- I respect others and I am respected by others
- I truly respect differences of opinion.
- I love and respect my body.

AFFIRMATIONS FOR WORTHINESS

- I am worthy of love and respect.
- I am worthy of success and happiness.
- I make a difference in the world.
- I have wonderful talents to share with the world.
- I am worthy of making my dreams come true.
- I have a great potential within me.
- I value my worth.
- I deserve having what I want.
- I am worthy of all good things.
- I am worthy of abundance.
- I am worthy of happiness.

AFFIRMATIONS TO BOOST SELF CONFIDENCE

- I love the person I am becoming.
- I am improving every day.
- I have power to change anything I want.
- I make good and wise decisions.
- I believe in myself and my abilities.
- I radiate with self confidence.
- Being confident comes easily to me.

AFFIRMATIONS FOR SELF DISCIPLINE

- All my choices are in agreement with my desires.
- All my habits are under my complete control.
- Every day I improve my willpower through persistent practice.
- Every day my willpower becomes stronger.
- Every moment of every day I am becoming more and more disciplined.
- Exercising self-control gives me an immense feeling of accomplishment
- I acknowledge my resistance and move forward anyway.

- I always do what I say I will do. My word is law in my life.
- I always follow through.
- I always put forth my best efforts into everything I do.
- I am above all temptations.
- I am fully in control of all that I do.
- I am in charge of my behaviors and actions.
- I am in charge of my life.
- I am in complete control of my thoughts, my actions, and my life.

AFFIRMATIONS TO LOVE YOUR INNER CHILD

- I respect my childlike innocence.
- I validate my inner child's thoughts and feelings.
- I love my inner child unconditionally.
- I re-parent my inner child with love, understanding and compassion.
- I listen to my inner child's needs.
- My inner child often has the right answer for me.
- I trust my inner child.
- I feel safe being innocent and vulnerable.

AFFIRMATIONS TO RECOVER YOUR INNER CHILD

- I will listen more and more to my inner child in the future.
- I will stop ignoring my inner child and pay more attention to it.
- I choose to embrace my inner child.
- It is okay to think differently than others.
- It is okay to feel differently than others.
- I am a strong person for showing my vulnerability.
- My inner child deserves to have a voice.

AFFIRMATIONS TO HEAL YOUR INNER CHILD

- I choose to let go of pain and focus on healing all aspects of my inner child.
- My inner child is not alone through the healing process.
- I give myself time to heal my inner child.
- My childhood does not define me and has no power over me anymore.
- I am thankful for all the ways my inner child has helped me to align with my true self.

SELF-LOVE & SELF-ESTEEM QUOTES

- "It's all about falling in love with yourself and sharing that love with someone who appreciates you, rather than looking for love to compensate for a self-love deficit." - Eartha Kitt

- To fall in love with yourself is the first secret to happiness. - Robert Morley

- The first place where self-esteem begins its journey is within us. — Stephen Richards

- What you think of yourself is much more important than what people think of you.

- Leave who you were. Love who you are. Look forward to who you will become.

- Don't think about what might go wrong. Think about what might go right.

- Never stop trying. Never stop believing. Never give up. Your day will come.

- Today is a beautiful day and I will attract good things into my life.

- Don't try to be perfect. Just try to be better than you were yesterday.

- Confidence is something you create in yourself by believing in who you are.

- You yourself, as much as anybody in the entire universe, deserve your love and affection -- Buddha.

- Love yourself first and everything else falls into line. You really have to love yourself to get anything done in this world. - Lucille Ball

- Look for something positive each day, even if you have to look a little harder, some days.

- Love who you are, embrace who you are. Love yourself. When you love yourself, people can kind of pick up on that: they can see confidence, they can see self-esteem, and naturally, people gravitate towards you. - Lilly Singh

- Avoid negative people, for they are the greatest destroyers of self confidence and self-esteem.

- Surround yourself with people who bring out the best in you.

- Staying positive does not mean that things will turn out okay. Rather it is knowing that you will be okay no matter how things turn out. - unknown

- Free yourself from your past mistakes, by forgiving yourself for what you have done or went through. Every day is another chance to start over.

- Remind yourself every day: I am in charge of my happiness. I will not let anything outside of myself control me.

- No matter who you are, no matter what you did, no matter where you've come from, you can always change, and become a better version of yourself. — Madonna

- Don't take negative people's comments to heart. Most of the time they're just saying what they think about themselves.

- Attitude is a choice. Happiness is a choice. Optimism is a choice. Kindness is a choice. Giving is a choice. Respect is a choice. Whatever choice you make makes you. Choose wisely. — Roy T. Bennett

- No one is in control of your happiness, but you ... therefore you have the power ... to change anything about yourself or your life that you want to change. - Barbara De Angelis

- You are loved, you have purpose, you are a masterpiece, you are wonderfully made, God has a great plan for you. --Germany Kent

Thank you

www.ingramcontent.com/pod-product-compliance
Lightning Source LLC
Chambersburg PA
CBHW020912080526
44589CB00011B/558